St. Mary R...
and...
South Amb...

TRIAL BY JURY

TRIAL BY JURY

BY JO KOLANDA AND JUDGE PATRICIA CURLEY

Franklin Watts/A First Book
New York/London/Toronto/Sydney/1988

Photograph courtesy of: Photo Researchers, Inc.: pp. 2 (Bill Bachman), 8 (Barbara Rios), 12 (Ray Ellis), 14 (J. Allan Cash), 30 (Porterfield Chickering), 31 (top, M. E. Warren; bottom, Spencer Grant), 32 (Bill Bachman), 34 (Richard Hutchings), 36 (Spencer Grant), 39 (Arthur Glauberman), 42 (Bill Bachman), 49 (Nancy J. Pierce), 53 (Barbara Rios), 54 (Thomas S. England), 58 (Bill Bachman), 62 (George E. Jones, III), 67 (Bruce Roberts), 74 (Arthur Glauberman), 75 (John Spragens, Jr.), 80 (Robert A. Clark); The Bettmann Archive: pp. 16, 19, 20 (bottom), 23, 25, 27, 70; New York Public Library Picture Collection: p. 20 (top); UPI/ Bettmann Newsphotos: p. 45.

Library of Congress Cataloging in Publication Data

Kolanda, Jo.
  Trial by jury / by Jo Kolanda and Patricia Curley.
    p.   cm.—(A First book)
  Summary: Examines jury trials, discussing their history, function, procedures, and significance in society.
    ISBN 0-531-10610-1
    1. Jury—United States—Juvenile literature. [1. Jury.]
I. Curley, Patricia. II. Title. III. Series.
KF8972.Z9K65   1988
347.73′752—dc19
[347.307752]   88-17008   CIP
                                          AC

Copyright © 1988 by Jo Kolanda and Patricia Curley
All rights reserved
Printed in the United States of America
5 4 3 2 1

CONTENTS

Chapter One
THE HISTORY OF
JURY TRIALS
9

Chapter Two
THE COURTROOM
29

Chapter Three
THE FUNCTION AND ROLE
OF A JURY TODAY
38

Chapter Four
CRIMINAL JURY TRIALS
52

Chapter Five
CIVIL JURY TRIALS
61

Chapter Six
WE THE JURY
69

Chapter Seven
SPECIAL USES OF THE JURY
82

GLOSSARY OF LEGAL TERMS
87

INDEX
93

TRIAL BY JURY

CHAPTER ONE

THE HISTORY OF JURY TRIALS

Americans are very interested in their country's legal system. A quick flip of the dial on daytime TV or a brief look at the latest movie releases is all that is needed to prove this.

One of the major components of our legal system is the jury trial. Generally speaking, a modern jury trial consists of a number of people selected at random who come to court, are questioned by lawyers to determine their fitness as a juror, listen to the formal presentation of evidence, examine the facts, and decide what is the truth.

This book is basically a study of jury trials and their history. However, before we begin let's take a look at how they fit into our system of government.

THE SEPARATION OF POWERS

Our government is made up of three branches: the executive branch, the legislative branch, and the judicial branch. Jury trials are only one facet of the judicial branch, or judiciary.

After the discovery of the New World, a wide variety of people came to our shores. Some came to find peace from religious persecution; others came believing that the new land would make them rich and powerful. The early settlers, with a wide assortment of life-styles and backgrounds, were fiercely independent. They soon came to resent English rule and felt exploited by the severe taxes levied upon them.

In 1787, after they had waged a successful war of independence against the English, representatives from each of the colonies met in Philadelphia for the so-called Constitutional Convention. The document they wrote, the Constitution, was quite brief by eighteenth-century standards, but it is the same document we live under today (although it now contains twenty-six Amendments, or additional clauses). It consists of nothing more than a set of rules that citizens of the United States have agreed to live by.

The Constitution established a federal (central) government. Besides allowing for the formation of a strong federal government, it also reserved certain rights for the colonies, or states. In some instances, the federal government and the state governments were to share power. Each state also has its own constitution, with some states giving themselves broader power than other states. Examples of shared power include the right to build roads, to collect taxes, and to protect the health and safety of citizens.

For the federal government, the founding fathers (women were excluded from power at the time) rejected a monarchy (a ruling family) and they were opposed to a dictatorship (absolute rule by one self-chosen leader). Thus they divided the government into the three separate branches, each with exclusive tasks. This relationship is called the *separation of powers.*

The executive branch is responsible for managing the country. The head of the executive branch is the president, whose duties include carrying out the law as well as making policy decisions on such matters as economics and relations with foreign governments. Two of the greatest powers the president has are to appoint federal judges and to veto laws made by the legislature. These powers to direct or thwart the actions of the other two branches of government are part of the system of so-called *checks and balances* that prevents any one branch from becoming too powerful. On the state level, the governor is the head of the executive branch. Local governments, which can be authorized by the state, often have a mayor as their executive head.

The legislative branch of our government is made up of two "houses," the House of Representatives and the Senate, collectively called Congress. Each state sends elected representatives to these houses, and it is the legislature's job to make laws. Every state, except Nebraska, has a legislative branch also made up of two houses. Cities often have so-called *city councils* to introduce new legislation.

Like the executive branch, the legislative branch of government was given certain powers to check the powers of the other branches. For example, Congress must confirm all of the president's appointments to the bench (judges) and is the only branch of government allowed to appropriate money (decide how taxes are to be spent).

The judicial branch of government is the most difficult branch to understand. It is the task of the judiciary to interpret (decide the meaning of) laws and decide if they are "constitutional," that is, in accordance with the rules laid out in the Constitution.

THE JUDICIARY

There are three levels of courts in the judiciary—federal, state, and local. On the federal level the judges who preside over trials

are called district judges. There are ninety-four districts within the United States. Someone who is unhappy with the result of his or her trial may "appeal" it to a federal Court of Appeals. These courts, numbering eleven around the country, hear cases as a panel. That is, several judges read over transcripts describing the events that occurred at the trial or written documents from the trial attorneys and determine whether the result was correct. If you are still unhappy with the outcome of your case, you can ask (petition) the Supreme Court of the United States to hear it. This court, the highest in the land, consists of nine justices. It listens to only a small percentage of petitioned cases. Unlike most state and local judges, federal judges are always appointed. They may serve until they retire or die.

As we have said, every state's constitution is unique. All states have a high court, though there are a variety of names it may go by. Many states have a middle court, similar to the federal Court of Appeals. Both the state supreme court and the state court of appeals hear appeals. Like their federal counterparts, they do not preside over cases. Their job is to decide whether the trial was conducted properly. The lowest level of state courts are also very different from state to state. In some states they are called circuit courts, in other states district courts. A judge may preside over only one kind of case, say criminal cases, or all kinds of cases, depending on the state. Depending on the state there are also several different procedures for selecting judges. Some are elected, some are appointed (usually by the governor).

The statue atop this court building represents justice. The scales are a symbol of justice.

The Supreme Court building in Washington, D.C., is the home of the Supreme Court of the United States.

Our court system, which relies heavily on juries to settle disputes, fits squarely into our Constitution's design of checks and balances. The courts not only interpret the laws but also strike down those that do not conform to our Constitution. In the courtroom, the jury represents the voice and will of the people and thus the jury system is itself a check against a court that is too powerful or against laws the people feel are unfair.

People in the United States believe in jury trials; the jury system is enormously popular in settling disputes. In fact, 80 to 90 percent of the jury trials in the world today take place in the United States.

Where did the idea for juries come from? How long have juries been in operation, and why do twelve people usually sit on a jury and not ten or fourteen? Why are only certain kinds of cases tried by a jury?

EARLY JURIES

Delving into the history of jury trials and their evolution requires one to look surprisingly far back into history. Although the exact origins of jury trials are not known, and historians frequently argue over this point, there is evidence supporting the view that the Egyptians had a type of jury system called the *Kenbet* more than four thousand years ago.

Archaeological finds also show that the ancient Greeks in Athens, centuries before the beginning of the Christian era, had a jury system of sorts called the *Ekklesia*. The "jury" was a loosely organized group of men who listened to the stories of both the accused and accusor. Since there were no formal rules in operation, the accused frequently spent more time telling of good deeds he or she had done and describing the many fine qualities he or she had than in relating the actual events. About 450 B.C., the Greeks developed specialized assemblies called *Dikasts,* whose

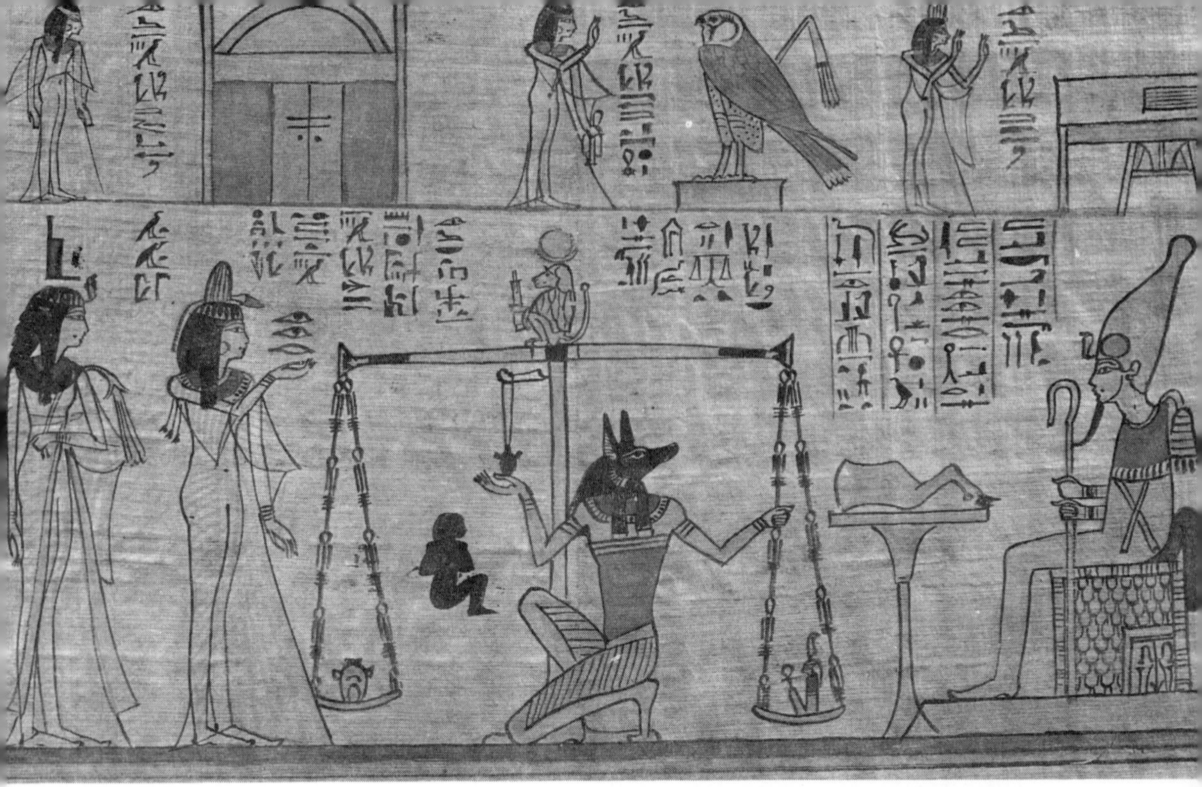

Top: a depiction drawn on papyrus, or paper, of an ancient Egyptian trial. Bottom: Justitia, goddess of justice.

only job was to decide disputes. Sometimes these assemblies had more than two hundred members; one could imagine that their discussions must have been quite lengthy!

Actually, to resolve disputes many civilizations developed systems (usually based on Roman law) that included some form of citizen participation. In ancient Norway men from different parts of the country were sent to the *gulathing,* where the *Logmann* (lawman) presided. Similar assemblies grew and matured in what is now modern-day Denmark, Sweden, Italy, and France. These early "juries," however, bore little resemblance to our contemporary juries. Some of the major differences were (1) early jurors were people who frequently had firsthand knowledge of the facts; (2) a unanimous verdict was not required; and (3) there were no rules establishing the number of jurors or how to present evidence.

The American jury is the direct descendent of the English system. The origins of the English jury, however, are not known for sure. Some historians believe that a form of jury was in existence by the time of the signing of the Magna Carta (the document signed by King John in 1215 promising certain rights to ordinary citizens). More recently, historians have come to believe that the English jury slowly evolved from the Frankish *inquisito,* brought to England by William the Conqueror when he won the Battle of Hastings in 1066. The *inquisito* was an order from the king requiring people to answer questions the king thought important. For example, he may have asked about the ownership of land in order to know how much to tax the people.

Before William the Conqueror imposed the *inquisito* on the English, they had a very different system. Anglo-Saxons (early inhabitants of England) were required to belong to a *tithing*. A tithing was a group of neighbors who helped each other but also made and enforced rules regarding the actions of individual members.

For example, if a member committed a crime, the tithing was responsible for bringing the person to justice. What passed for justice at this time was a requirement that the guilty person or his or her tithing pay the victim or any relatives or heirs a set sum of money.

Eventually, the ruling monarch sent out judges to monitor the disputes of English inhabitants and to preside over what were then very rudimentary "trials." Although these early trials were designed to resolve disputes, they bore little resemblance to modern trials. In the early English courts the methods of presenting evidence and decision-making were drastically different from what they are now. They included: (1) the giving of an oath; (2) compurgation; (3) official witnesses; and (4) the ordeal.

In minor cases the accused had to swear to tell the truth. This is a custom that has survived into the twentieth century. In more serious cases, a person would sometimes be required to get other people to take an oath with him or her. These people, called *compurgators,* would lend you their oath and swear you were telling the truth.

A third type of evidence was the "official witness." Official witnesses played a role similar to today's notary public. They would witness official acts and then be available to testify.

But to truly understand the realities of eleventh-century justice, we must explore the form of proof called the *ordeal* to realize how terrifying life could be at this point in history and to appreciate how far civilization has progressed.

The ordeal was a truth-seeking device. Trial by ordeal was used in the tenth, eleventh, and twelfth centuries, with some forms lasting until the thirteenth century. The ordeal had as its origin a belief that God could be called upon to help in "divining" the truth. The ordeal was used primarily for people accused of serious crimes and it was used only when the other methods of proof were not available. It operated by asking the accused to perform some

Two trials in medieval England, one inside a courtroom, the other, outside. The trial held outside is under the town's oak tree. The defendant is pleading his own case.

taking an oath before a notary

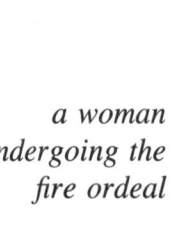

a woman undergoing the fire ordeal

extremely difficult—if not impossible—act. Among those ordeals in use were the *fire ordeal,* the *water ordeal, corsnaed,* and *wager of battle,* although there were other forms that were specially fashioned for certain crimes.

The fire ordeal meant a person accused of a crime had to walk over a hot fire. The theory was that God would not let an innocent person suffer any burns.

For the water ordeal the accused had to put part of his or her body in boiling water. As with the fire ordeal, the accused could not suffer any burns. Sometimes the accused was instead thrown into a large river or lake. It was believed that the guilty would float and the innocent would sink. (It is not clear how long you had to stay underwater to prove your innocence!)

With the corsnaed ordeal, you had to swallow a large morsel. If you were innocent, you supposedly would not choke.

As might be expected, the vast majority of people involved in this process were found guilty. Frequently, the only fate awaiting a person who failed these brutal and painful tests was to have a foot cut off, or, possibly, be put to death. Your "sentence" depended on the gravity of the offense.

Another form of deciding disputes that had little to do with finding the truth and a lot to do with physical agility was the wager of battle, introduced to England by the Normans (William the Conqueror). Bareheaded and barearmed, except for long sticks, the two conflicting parties would attempt to kill each other or get the opponent to give up by saying "craven." If neither of these things happened, the fight would end when the sun set.

Obviously, the various ordeals did not provide a very satisfying legal system. So in time the king established a more formal system. Courts would meet at set times, and people could take their disputes to be heard before juries. In these early juries the jurors were people who knew something about the facts. This contrasts with today's jury, where knowing anything about the facts could disqualify you from serving. Also, the use of *pleadings* or *legal documents* was quite limited. Pleadings are formal written statements describing the positions of the parties (sides) in a lawsuit. Legal documents are written materials that can be introduced as evidence in a trial, for example, a deed or a will.

Sometime in the fourteenth century, the "witness" jurors were replaced by disinterested parties. Thus, modern jurors evolved from people who were actually witnesses to people who were selected because they knew nothing about the facts.

The transition to a jury system was not an abrupt one. In the thirteenth century, an accused person had to agree to be tried by a jury. Frequently, a guilty person would not consent to a trial. The guilty reasoned that life in jail, although unpleasant, was a far better fate than having a trial. They recognized that a trial would almost always result in a conviction and a conviction in the penalty of death, since, in this era, there existed none of the safeguards found in our present criminal justice system to protect the innocent—including the accused's right to an attorney and the prohibition against the use of force to exact a confession, to name just two. To make matters worse, laws were passed inflicting severe punishments on those who refused a jury. In addition, harshness was reserved not only for the person on trial. It was customary to withhold food and water from jurors while they deliberated. Often jurors were not allowed even to go to the bathroom. The prevailing wisdom was that this would aid in the jury reaching a swift and fair decision.

a German courtroom scene, around the turn of the sixteenth century

Sometimes jurors could themselves be indicted in a process called *attaint*. This was a system whereby a second jury would be called upon to look at the evidence viewed by the first jury and see if it had come to the correct decision. If it hadn't, the jurors in the first trial would be fined or imprisoned.

About a century later, twelve seems to have been established as the number of jurors used in a standard trial, although there would be much experimentation later. Some believe that the number twelve was selected because of the twelve apostles or, possibly, the twelve tribes of Israel. The fourteenth century was also the time when the unanimous verdict was introduced in criminal cases. Before then, a simple majority could convict someone.

By the seventeenth century jury trials had become fairly regulated. The right to a jury trial was guaranteed by law and not subject to the whims of the reigning monarch. Jurors were selected from the surrounding community and were chosen via a system that allowed each side to reject certain jurors. Unlike in earlier days, jurors, while serving, were kept apart from others and were not allowed to talk to the witnesses or the involved parties.

The English settlers arriving on the shores of North America brought with them the concept of a jury trial. Since so many of the English colonists who came to the United States did so because they were being persecuted in England by the monarch, the right to a jury trial was important to them.

As the colonies prospered, many people became disenchanted with the English monarchy. They felt the English should stay out of the internal politics of the colonies, and the jury trial became, in many instances, a way of expressing this belief. In several col-

a colonial trial

onies, juries refused to convict people accused of political crimes against the English government despite overwhelming evidence.

THE MODERN JURY COMES OF AGE

The fact that the jury system, decreasing in use everywhere else in the world, has enjoyed such popularity in the United States is probably due, in part, to our country's early experience of using the jury to wrest power from an oppressive government. The deep respect in this country for the jury system is founded on the belief that jury trials can prevent the government from getting too powerful and also prevent, or at least hinder, the enforcement of unfair laws. Since jurors, unlike judges, do not have to explain their verdicts or give reasons for acquitting (freeing) someone, they play the role of the conscience of the community. Juries have proven themselves over time to be an effective and humane system for resolving disputes.

Not only do the U.S. Constitution and the Amendments to the Constitution make mention of a right to a jury trial, but most state constitutions do, too. Today, a person is entitled to a jury in any matter which, under common law (an unwritten body of law based on the customs and laws in England), gives a person a right to a jury trial. Also, state laws have been passed guaranteeing the right to a jury trial in certain types of cases. This helps explain why, in this country, a person is not entitled to a jury in a divorce case or a case determining heirs when someone dies, since these types of cases under common law do not allow a jury.

Despite the long-standing historical success of juries, and the important part they have played in maintaining a balance of power, there are people who believe they are archaic and may actually impede justice. Author Mark Twain once said, "The jury system

A jury discusses the evidence during a court recess.

puts a ban upon intelligence and honesty, and a premium upon ignorance, stupidity and perjury. It is a shame that we must continue to use a worthless system because it was good a thousand years ago."

Some modern scholars criticize the use of juries in certain technical cases because they believe the amount of specialized knowledge needed to make an intelligent decision is simply beyond the ability of the average juror. For instance, in deciding cases in which medical doctors are accused of negligence (carelessness), the jurors need to know and understand what other doctors would do in the same circumstances. This is difficult for people who have had little formal education.

Some feel that the use of juries in criminal cases is an expensive luxury our society can no longer afford. The recruitment—that is, the selection and payment—of jurors is an enormous drain on already tight government budgets, to say nothing of the cost of the judge, court staff, and attorneys. Of great concern, too, are the delays caused by special jury requests and the absolute right of every accused person to have a jury trial even if he or she is already serving a life sentence or three hundred years' worth of jail time.

Occasionally, too, although rarely, jurors will act on prejudice or bias and bring in an unfair verdict. More disturbing is the fact that there is no uniformity to jury verdicts. Identical situations can produce different verdicts in different places. Despite these criticisms, juries appear to be here to stay, in our federal court system as well as in all fifty states.

CHAPTER TWO

THE COURTROOM

Jury trials are almost always held in an officially designated courtroom, typically in a county courthouse or public safety building, a federal government building, or a city or village hall. A tour of these various buildings throughout your state would probably show you a wide range of different atmospheres but very similar participants and procedures.

Many courtrooms are large and elegant, filled with wood paneling and elaborately carved woodwork. They radiate an awesome sense of tradition and power. Newer courtrooms, built to accommodate an ever-expanding court system, will probably be smaller, more modern, and convey a sense of businesslike efficiency. Courtrooms that handle a large volume of criminal cases often leave a visitor with an impression of chaos. They may intimidate those of us who are not a regular part of the court system.

Perhaps the most noticeable feature of all courtrooms is a partition that clearly separates the "insiders" from the "outsiders." Lawyers walk confidently through the gate in the partition, while

A traditional (top) and a more modern-looking courtroom (bottom). Although they look different, both serve the cause of justice.

The partition is in the foreground, and the judge's desk, elevated, is in the background. At this point in the trial, a conference is being held at the judge's bench.

those waiting for their case to be called usually sit timidly in the section in the back, sometimes called the *gallery*. Normally the gallery has rows of benches or chairs for the general public.

In the front of the courtroom is the *bench,* or judge's desk. It is usually the largest piece of furniture in the room and is also usually raised above floor level. In many courtrooms, when the judge enters the room to begin official court business, a court official will loudly announce, "All rise. This court is now in session," signaling all present to stand up and show respect for the power and authority of our court system, which the judge symbolizes.

When a federal or state court is in session, or conducting official court business, you will also see a *court reporter,* whose job it is to take down all that is said. The court reporter sits close to the bench and takes down in a special shorthand all of the *testimony,* or official remarks, on a small machine called a stenograph. An official written record of the court proceeding, called a *transcript,* can be made from this. Many local courts tape-record their sessions and keep the tapes for a brief time, in case questions come up about what happened.

The *court clerk* usually sits right in front of or next to the judge. He or she is responsible for all of the necessary paperwork and record keeping that goes along with the court business. For example, the clerk keeps track of when cases are scheduled and types letters and reports for the judge.

Many courts also have a *bailiff.* Criminal courts usually have more than one. A bailiff is a uniformed law enforcement officer who is in charge of security and order in the courtroom. The bailiff makes sure people behave in an orderly and respectful manner and escorts them out of the room if they do not. In courts that hear criminal cases, the bailiffs bring prisoners to and from the jail and the courtroom for their court appearances.

A little farther back from the judge's bench are usually two tables where the lawyers for each side sit. If the case involves a criminal charge, the *prosecutor* and the police officer in charge of the investigation sit at one table. The crime victim does not sit at the prosecutor's table in most states because criminal cases are brought in the name of the state versus the *defendant* (person accused of committing the crime); the victim is not a "party." The defendant sits at the other table with his or her attorney, called the *defense attorney*. For defendants who are too poor to afford a private attorney, the defense attorney is often a *public defender* appointed by and paid for by the state or federal government. If the case involves a civil lawsuit, the *plaintiff*, or person who started the action, sits at one table, with the defendant (the person being sued in this case) at the other table.

Many courtrooms also contain a *jury box*, or special seating area near the judge where the jury sits while hearing testimony during a trial. The jury box usually has twelve chairs in two rows of six each, one raised behind the other, as are seats in a sporting arena.

Right next to the judge and in clear view of the jury is the *witness stand*, or chair where witnesses sit while they testify. Much of the evidence presented to juries comes from witnesses answering the questions of lawyers while they sit on the witness stand. During a trial the lawyers on each side of the case will call as many witnesses as they need to prove all the facts in their case.

As a young man on the witness stand answers the attorney's questions, the court reporter takes down the testimony on a stenograph.

When the lawyer who called the witness is asking questions, it is called *direct examination*. When the other lawyer questions that witness, it is called *cross examination*. The *testimony,* or answers the witnesses give, is used to help the jury reach a verdict.

Lawyers must phrase their questions based on certain rules called the *rules of evidence*. The other side is free to challenge a question or the admission of a piece of evidence at any time by making an *objection*. If the judge decides that the question was proper, he or she will *overrule* the objection and tell the witness to answer the question. If the judge rules that the objection is *sustained,* the lawyer must withdraw the question. Sometimes, in these disputes, the judge will tell the jury to disregard certain testimony and to "strike" it from the record. This means that when making their decision the jurors must put out of their minds something they have already heard during the trial.

Judges usually have private offices, called *chambers,* next to the courtroom, in which they conduct private meetings with lawyers or others. There is also usually a *jury room,* to which the jury must go to *deliberate* (make their decision on the case). Jurors also "retire" to the jury room if the judge wishes to discuss something with the lawyers that the jury should not hear. Courts that handle criminal cases also have a *lockup,* or small jail cell, for prisoners who are waiting to appear in court.

Top: *prosecuting and defending attorneys during a court recess in a murder trial.* Bottom: *the jurors sit in the jury box, listening to the testimony of a witness.*

CHAPTER THREE

THE FUNCTION AND ROLE OF A JURY TODAY

It's not often that average people get a chance to do something really important for their country. Being a juror gives one that chance.

The citizens chosen to serve as jurors in the nation's courts are given enormous power and responsibility. They must uphold the most basic of American values. We rely on juries every day to hear both sides of a story and to decide what is true, what is fair, and what is just, in spite of their own personal feelings.

The U.S. Constitution, in Article III, states: "The trial of all crimes, except in cases of impeachment, shall be by jury; and such trial shall be held in the state where the said crimes shall have been committed. . . ." The Sixth Amendment to the Constitution adds: "In all criminal prosecutions, the accused shall enjoy the right to a speedy and public trial, by an impartial jury of the State and district wherein the crime shall have been committed. . . ."

When people are accused of having committed a crime, they

You would report to this building if you were a resident of New York City and were selected to serve on jury duty.

face questioning and arrest by the police, possibly spending time in a jail, and being formally "charged" and then prosecuted by the state. If they are convicted (found guilty) by a jury of having committed the crime, they face the possibility of losing what is most dear to all of us—our freedom.

The states have extended the right to a jury trial in many civil (noncriminal) cases. For example, they have acknowledged that when a person is sued, he or she should have the right to a jury trial to be protected against wrongfully being deprived of money or property.

It is important that courts be able to conduct jury trials on any given day. Therefore, groups of citizens are sent special notices, called *summonses*, telling them that they must appear in court on a certain day and be prepared to serve on a jury. If a person who receives a summons to jury duty does not appear when ordered, he or she can be fined or even jailed.

Some states, in an effort to make it easier for people to serve on juries, have passed laws to protect workers who are summoned. For example, employers cannot fire someone if he or she misses work because of jury duty, and, in many places, the company must pay that person regular wages while the person is on jury duty.

What a jury does and how it does it varies according to the kind of case to be decided. Even the number of people who sit on the jury depends on what case it will hear. However, some things are basic to all juries.

With few exceptions, jury trials are open to the public. Anyone can sit in a courtroom and listen to a case being presented to a jury. (This is not true, however, in cases involving a juvenile accused of committing a crime; those trials are usually closed to public observers.)

The people who are chosen to be on a jury take a formal oath. They swear that they will listen to all of the evidence presented

CLERK OF CIRCUIT COURT
MILWAUKEE COUNTY COURTHOUSE
901 N. 9TH STREET
MILWAUKEE, WISCONSIN 53233

FIRST CLASS MAIL
U.S. POSTAGE
PAID 1 OZ
MILWAUKEE, WIS
PERMIT 1630

JURY SUMMONS
ISSUED TO:

YOU ARE HEREBY ORDERED TO REPORT OR CALL TO SERVE A TERM OF JURY SERVICE AT THE DATE, TIME, AND LOCATION SHOWN. FAILURE TO RESPOND AS ORDERED IS PUNISHABLE BY A FINE.

YOUR SUMMONS IS FOR SERVICE AS A:

UNLESS THE TRIAL FOR WHICH YOU ARE SERVING LASTS LONGER, YOUR TERM OF SERVICE WILL NOT EXTEND BEYOND THIS DATE

YOUR REPORTING LOCATION, UNLESS YOU ARE INSTRUCTED OTHERWISE, IS:

CLERK OF CIRCUIT COURT, JURY ASSEMBLY, ROOM 630, 6TH FLOOR
MILWAUKEE COUNTY COURTHOUSE
901 N. 9TH STREET, MILWAUKEE, WISCONSIN

SAVE THIS PORTION FOR YOUR RECORDS

------- DETACH SUMMONS HERE -------

RETURN THIS PORTION PER STATE STATUTE 756

YOU ARE ORDERED UNDER WISCONSIN STATE STATUTE 756.04(2)(B) TO COMPLETE AND RETURN THIS PORTION OF THE SUMMONS WITHIN 10 DAYS OF ITS RECEIPT. FAILURE TO DO SO OR WILLFUL MISREPRESENTATION OF ANY MATERIAL FACT ON THIS SUMMONS MAY RESULT IN A FINE OF NOT MORE THAN $500.00.

1. ARE YOU A CITIZEN OF THE UNITED STATES? ____ YES ____ NO
2. ARE YOU AT LEAST 18 YEARS OF AGE? ____ YES ____ NO
3. CAN YOU READ AND UNDERSTAND THE ENGLISH LANGUAGE? ____ YES ____ NO
4. DO YOU CURRENTLY LIVE WITHIN MILWAUKEE COUNTY? ____ YES ____ NO
5. HAVE YOU BEEN SUMMONED FOR JURY SERVICE IN MILWAUKEE COUNTY WITHIN THE LAST TWO YEARS?
   IF YES, THE DATE OF SERVICE WAS .... ____ YES ____ NO
6. ARE YOU NOW A PARTY IN A LAWSUIT IN MILWAUKEE COUNTY? ____ YES ____ NO
7. ARE YOU A CONVICTED FELON WHOSE CIVIL RIGHTS HAVE NOT BEEN RESTORED? ____ YES ____ NO

IF YOUR ANSWER TO ANY QUESTION FROM NO. 1 TO NO. 4 WAS "NO" OR IF YOUR RESPONSE TO ANY QUESTION FROM NO. 5 TO NO. 7 WAS "YES" YOU ARE DISQUALIFIED AS A JUROR, AND YOU DO NOT HAVE TO REPORT. BUT, YOU MUST STILL **RETURN THIS PORTION.** ALL OTHER JURORS REPORT ON SUMMONED DATE.

IF THERE IS ANY OTHER REASON **WHY** YOU SHOULD NOT BE REQUIRED TO REPORT AS SUMMONED, PLEASE INDICATE THAT REASON BELOW SO THAT A JUDGE CAN REVIEW IT! A REPLY WILL BE MAILED ONE WEEK BEFORE YOUR SUMMONED DATE.

_____
_____
_____

MY OCCUPATION IS _____

MY MAILING ADDRESS HAS BEEN CHANGED TO:
(NO P.O. BOX NUMBERS)

MY TELEPHONE NUMBERS ARE:
HOME _____
WORK _____

I HEREBY CERTIFY THAT THE ABOVE INFORMATION IS COMPLETE AND TRUE.

SIGNED _____ DATE _____

A jury summons

A witness swears to tell the truth. Both jurors and witnesses take a formal oath.

during the trial and that their decisions will be based solely on that evidence. They swear they will try to be fair and impartial and that they will not let any personal prejudices influence their decisions.

Asking people to take this formal oath is asking for a real commitment. Jurors must promise to devote their full attention and concern to the problems and fate of someone they don't even know. They must promise to search their own souls for possible prejudice. For example, do they wrongly believe minorities are more likely to commit crimes than white people? Do they hate police officers? Do they think insurance companies try to cheat people? And, if they must admit to themselves that they have certain biases, can they honestly say they will rise above them? They must promise that they will be fair and impartial when they consider the evidence they hear and see. If they cannot promise they will be fair, they should not serve on the jury.

For example, Ann Dearborn's ten-year-old son, David, was killed five years ago by a drunk driver. The pain of missing him is still very great. Today, Ann is sitting in a courtroom with other prospective jurors. The lawyers are in the process of picking a jury (called *impaneling*) to hear a case against a man charged with drunken driving. "Could I listen to this case with an open mind?" Ann asks herself. "I know this is not the man who killed David, but will I be able to be fair? Will my anger and sadness because of David affect how I judge the man in this courtroom?" Ann struggles with her feelings. "Yes. I will be able to put my feelings aside and listen with an open mind," she decides.

All juries assume the role we normally think of as being that of a judge. The jury is the "trier of the facts." First it listens to the lawyers' opening statements. In these, the lawyers for each side tell the jury what they think the evidence will show. Then the jury listens to witnesses tell what they know about the case to the lawyers on both sides, who ask them questions. The jury may also examine physical evidence, such as photographs, weapons, or other objects. In some cases, a court official will read a statement—called a *deposition*—that was made earlier by a witness who will not appear during the trial. Or, the jury may watch a videotaped deposition on a television screen. Videotaped depositions are most often used in civil cases in which it would be extremely inconvenient for the witness to appear at the trial. They are used in some states in criminal cases involving children who are witnesses. The children can testify soon after the crime and in a place that is more comfortable for a child than a courtroom.

In some cases, jurors are taken out of the courtroom for a "jury view." For example, in a criminal case, they may go to examine the scene of the crime. In a civil case, they may go to see a piece of machinery that injured someone. Jurors may also hear evidence that will not be discussed during the trial. For instance, they may get "judicial notice" of facts that are not in dispute. As an example, the jury may hear that on April 22, 1987, at 8:30 p.m., in Chicago, Illinois, the temperature was 45 degrees, and it was raining. Official weather records can document this fact. Jurors also hear "stipulations" of facts that will not be argued. For example, both lawyers arguing a murder trial may agree to stipulate that Allison Petrovick was the murder victim. That agreement means that Allison's mother, who went to the morgue to identify her body, will not have to go through the pain of reliving that moment in court. In some cases, jurors will hear direct evidence (i.e., Jessica White testified that she actually saw Joshua Britton stepping through the jeweler's broken window with several rings in his hand). However, sometimes evidence is *circumstantial,* as when there are no eyewitnesses. For example, Joshua Britton's fingerprint was found on the inside of the jewelry store window and a man matching Britton's description was seen

Members of a jury examine the scene of a crime, a murder committed in a park.

in a pawnshop selling several rings later identified as some of the stolen merchandise.

Overall, a jury's job is to listen carefully and weigh both sides of a case. But there are some facts that a jury will not be allowed to hear because the information might make them prejudiced against one side. For example, a civil jury may not know if a defendant had been convicted of a crime related to, or unrelated to, the facts they will hear. Take the case of John Sanders, who was driving the car that hit Peter Thompson. Peter was hurt very badly and is now confined to a wheelchair. John Sanders was convicted last year of the crime of causing serious bodily harm while driving under the influence of alcohol. Today, Peter Thompson is suing John for hundreds of thousands of dollars in damages to pay for his medical expenses, his pain and suffering, and for lost wages because he can no longer work at the construction job he had before he was injured. A jury will decide if John caused Peter's injuries and damages, but they will not know that John has been convicted of the criminal charges.

In a criminal case a jury would also not get to hear evidence that was obtained illegally. For example, when the police arrested Mike Hanson for burglary, they were required by law to "read him his rights." One of those rights is the right to remain silent and have an attorney present while he answered any questions. But the officer who arrested Mike did not inform him of his rights before he questioned him about the burglary. Mike confessed, but

This suspect was read his rights by the arresting officer and then put in jail to await trial.

when his case was tried by a jury, the judge excluded mention of the confession and the jurors did not hear about it.

Finally, at the end of the presentations, the jury hears closing arguments and jury instructions. The lawyers for each side get a chance to argue, or tell the jurors what conclusions they think the jury should draw and why. In their closing arguments, they sum up everything the jury has seen and heard and then try to persuade the jurors why they should agree with their side. Then the judge instructs the jury in the law, a process sometimes called *charging the jury*. That is, the judge tells the jury what laws apply to the case. For example, the judge might explain which driver had the right-of-way in an automobile accident, what the law says about the duty of a landowner toward an uninvited guest, or how the law defines "self defense." It is then left to the jury to decide which witnesses are telling the truth and what physical evidence is important.

But every jury is made up of individuals. Each individual must make his or her own personal assessment of the facts presented. Jurors are told that, while serving, they may not talk about the case to anyone, including other jurors, until the presentation of the case is finished.

Sometimes jury trials end unexpectedly. This is because the jury has heard or seen something that they should not have. For example, a judge would have to declare a *mistrial* if jurors heard anyone testify that John Sanders had already been convicted of a crime for injuring Peter Thompson, or that Mike Hanson confessed to the burglary. When a mistrial is declared, the trial ends. Both sides have to start all over with a brand-new jury. Usually, though, juries hear an entire case and never hear facts that the judge has decided might prejudice the jurors one way or the other.

Keeping facts from a jury is very controversial. Some people feel it is essential to protect juries from prejudice. Others think

During a trial the judge must instruct the jury in the law. The thick, dark notebook shown here on the judge's desk contains jury instructions for criminal cases.

that jurors should be trusted to be fair in weighing *all* the facts, even if some things "look bad" for one side or the other.

Tom Sanders was being tried on a charge of first-degree murder for a death that occurred in Oklahoma eleven years ago. Tom, and most of the witnesses in the case, lived in Texas. Several of the witnesses had told the police soon after the crime was committed that Tom was with them, in Texas, at the time and therefore could not have committed the murder. During the trial, the jurors heard those witnesses testify that they had lied because they were afraid of the defendant. One witness, George Redding, testified that he drove Tom to Oklahoma; that he waited in the car while the murder was committed; and that Tom showed him the body of the woman and said, "That's what will happen to you if you don't give me an alibi." Tom got on the witness stand and said that George killed the woman.

The jurors learned that Tom had a criminal record but didn't know for what kinds of crimes. They deliberated for several days. They finally found the defendant guilty. After they delivered their verdict, the jurors learned that Tom had recently been convicted of first-degree murder and attempted murder and had been sentenced to death in Texas. The reason that witnesses came forward to testify after eleven years was that they finally felt safe. Many of the jurors were angry that they didn't know all of the facts.

Usually, members of a jury sit in the jury box during the course of a trial and merely listen to the lawyers' opening statements, to witnesses' testimony, and to the lawyers' closing arguments before they begin to discuss the case. But, in very complicated cases, the judge may allow the jurors to take notes during the trial and to ask questions after both sides have finished presenting evidence. If jurors have questions, they usually can't just raise their hands in the courtroom and ask them. They must wait until they are in the jury room, write out the questions, and give them to the bailiff, who gives them to the judge. The judge then decides how to respond to the jury's questions.

More recently, some judges have experimented in allowing jurors to ask their own questions of a witness. Many jurors feel this helps them in their deliberations and makes the decision making easier.

After the case is finished being presented, the jurors are escorted by deputy sheriffs to a special room near the court, where they will begin their discussion, or deliberations. They will discuss what they have seen and heard, but only with their fellow jurors; the judge orders them not to talk to anyone else about the case. But, before deliberating, the jurors may vote to elect one member of the group the *foreperson,* or leader. (Sometimes the foreperson is simply the first juror chosen to sit on the jury.) This leader will be responsible for keeping the deliberations going and for keeping order in the group. The foreperson may have the difficult job of telling someone to stop interrupting other jurors or of encouraging someone who is very shy to voice an opinion. The leader also calls for a vote to see if the members of the jury have reached a verdict and speaks for the jury when it returns to court to inform the judge of its verdict.

CHAPTER FOUR

CRIMINAL JURY TRIALS

A criminal case does not involve one person accusing another of doing something wrong. Rather, it is the state that accuses and prosecutes a suspected criminal. For example, someone snatched Martha Williams' purse. Robert Ellerson was arrested and charged with robbery. The criminal case is called the *State of Wisconsin* v *Robert Ellerson*, not *Martha Williams* v *Robert Ellerson*. Our government has decided that a crime hurts not only the crime victim but also the entire community, so a criminal prosecution is made in the name of every citizen in the state.

A jury that will decide a criminal case usually has twelve members, and they must reach a unanimous decision. If even one person does not agree with the decision of the other eleven, the jury cannot deliver a verdict. When a judge is convinced that the members of a jury have had enough time to thoroughly consider and discuss all of the evidence before them, but that they are unable to come to a unanimous decision (a situation sometimes called a *hung,* or *deadlocked, jury*), the judge must declare a mistrial.

Across the country, in courthouses like this one, criminal cases are tried every day.

A teen jury votes on the sentence of a teenager who has pleaded guilty to a misdemeanor, a lesser crime. In this voluntary program, the teen jury listens to testimony, receives instructions from a judge (foreground), and votes to determine the sentences of other teens who have pleaded guilty to misdemeanors and agreed to go before a jury of their peers.

Jurors that are judging the facts presented in a criminal trial must make their decisions based on the highest *burden of proof* required of any jury. They must decide whether, based on the evidence, they believe that the defendant is guilty "beyond a reasonable doubt." If after they weigh all the evidence, they feel that a reasonable person would not be convinced that the defendant committed the crime, they must find the accused person not guilty. But if, after they add up the facts, they feel certain that the defendant did commit the crime, they must vote for a verdict of guilty.

A jury heard the following facts: Alfred and Barney Smith were charged with armed robbery for allegedly forcing Marc Westin, at gunpoint, to give them all of the money in the cash register of the gas station at which Marc worked nights. Both men wore ski masks so Marc could not see their faces. When the men ran out of the gas station, Larry Denton thought they looked suspicious and wrote down the license plate number of their car. Marc pressed an alarm button as soon as the two robbers left, and police arrived soon afterward. Larry Denton gave the license number and a description of the car to the officers. A few minutes later, two other officers spotted the car from the description on their car radios; they pulled up to the car in question just as two men got out. The officers placed the men under arrest and searched the vehicle. They found a gun and $350 in cash. No ski masks. Both men were wearing blue jeans and dark wool jackets.

Marc testified that he could not identify their faces but said that the men who held him up were wearing jeans and dark jackets. He also said he thought the cash register had about $300 in it when it was robbed. The defendants testified that they had won the money found in their car in a pool game, that they had stopped at the gas station to use the bathroom, and that they didn't know anything about a robbery or how a gun got in their car. A friend of the defendants testified that she saw them win $350 in a pool game and that she was sure they didn't own a gun. The defense attorney told the jury that the two men were victims of bad timing; that they had been framed by the real robbers, who threw the gun in their car; and that, because the victim couldn't positively identify them, the jury could not find them guilty beyond a reasonable doubt. The jury had to decide which witnesses to believe and to use common sense in deciding the case.

Some criminal cases get a lot of publicity, with the media carrying reports of nearly everything that happens in the case. These cases present special problems for juries. Jurors must swear an oath that they will not be influenced by anything other than the evidence they hear and see in the courtroom. But a reporter can print or broadcast opinions or facts that will never be presented to a jury. Thus, news reports about a crime or about a defendant could easily influence someone's feelings about whether the defendant is guilty or not before the trial even starts. Sometimes the judge must take special precautions in picking a jury.

GANG MEMBER TELLS OF PLOT IN DOUBLE MURDER

This headline was printed in the daily newspaper of a small city shortly after two people were murdered. Every day the paper reported on the crime and on the man who was accused of the murders. Such serious crimes were rare in the city, and most people who lived there followed the news reports closely. Much of what was reported in the news would never be presented to the jury that eventually heard the case.

A defense attorney who is defending someone accused of committing a highly publicized crime may ask the judge for a *change of venue,* or new place of trial. The defense attorney argues to the judge that the defendant probably can't get a fair trial because of the difficulty in selecting a fair and impartial jury from people who live in the area and who have been exposed to much of the pretrial publicity. If the judge agrees, the defense attorney may order that the trial be held in another city, where there hasn't been so much publicity.

That decision, however, can cause a great deal of hardship for everyone involved in the case. For instance, witnesses may be required to travel long distances in order to testify. The prosecutor and defense attorney would have to be away from their homes and offices for days or weeks. Thus, some judges decide to have the trial in their own courtroom but bring in a jury from another city. The jurors are chosen from a town or city that hasn't heard a lot about the case. Only the jurors must travel in order to participate in the trial. Many judges feel that this is the fairest thing to do, because the jury will be *sequestered,* or kept apart from everyone else anyway, even during the presentation of the case. Jurors are usually sequestered whenever they will be deciding a case that is likely to be in the news during the trial—a first-degree murder case, for example. Sequestered jurors must stay together during the trial and for the entire time it takes them to deliberate, or decide, the case. They are carefully protected from any outside contact with family or friends or news reports of the case they will decide. One or two bailiffs escort them to and from the courtroom wherever they go—when they go to the jury room to wait or deliberate, when they go for meals, even when they go to their hotel at night to sleep.

A trial that lasts for many weeks can be very hard on a sequestered juror. The bailiffs who are guarding the jurors try to arrange entertainment for them during the hours and days when they are not hearing testimony or deliberating. If their hotel has a pool, one of the bailiffs may take jurors who like to swim to it. On weekends, they may go to the zoo or to a ballgame, as long as the judge approves the cost.

In a criminal case, if the defendant is found guilty, the jury

A prosecuting attorney shows a piece of evidence to the witness.

may still not be finished with its work. In a few states, it is the jury that sentences the convicted defendant to a prison term or determines how much restitution (payment) should be ordered for the victim.

In states that have a *death penalty* for certain crimes, the jury that returns a guilty verdict against someone accused of such a crime will then be asked to decide whether the defendant should be sentenced to prison or to death. The prosecutor who wants a sentence of death presents evidence and arguments to jurors to try to convince them that the defendant should die for what he or she did. For instance, the prosecutor may ask witnesses to testify as to the character of the defendant and may mention additional criminal acts of the defendant.

The jury convicted Ralph Avery of first-degree murder for killing his girlfriend, Lisa. The defense attorney told the jurors that Ralph had been rejected by his mother when he was a child and that his girlfriend had started seeing another man and was about to break off their relationship. He said Ralph was truly sorry now, and the jurors saw Ralph crying as he listened to his attorney. The prosecutor told the jury of Ralph's previous crimes. Police officers testified that Ralph had been convicted of sexual assault in the past. A prisoner who shared a cell with Ralph before the trial testified that Ralph bragged about how easy it was to kill a woman and how easy it was to "beat the system." The jurors returned to the jury room to decide whether to sentence Ralph to prison or death. They chose prison.

Some people accused of committing a crime enter a special plea that means a jury will have to decide first whether they committed the crime and then, if they did, whether they should be held accountable for their actions. In these cases, the jury hears evidence on the facts of the case and returns to court with a verdict. If that verdict is guilty, the jury then hears testimony from doctors, who give their opinions about the defendant's mental condition at the time the crime was committed. If the jury decides the defendant was sane, the judge can sentence him or her to prison. If the jury's decision is that the defendant was insane, the judge must place the defendant in the custody of a mental health treatment facility.

Maryanne Jones was convicted by a jury of first-degree murder for drowning her newborn boy in the bathtub. After the verdict, the defense attorney called two psychiatrists to the witness stand. Maryanne had a long history of mental illness and had spent many years in a mental hospital. She claimed that God told her he had wanted her to kill the baby because it was the son of the devil. The prosecutor called Maryanne's sister, who testified that Maryanne was very upset when she got pregnant because it meant that she would not be able to finish college the following year. He then argued that, because Maryanne planned in advance how to kill the baby, she was sane at the time. Maryanne leaned over the table in front of her and sobbed during the entire hearing. The jurors then went out of the courtroom to discuss whether Maryanne was mentally responsible when she killed her child. They decided she wasn't.

Every juror who hears a criminal case has a heavy responsibility. He or she must listen carefully throughout the case presentation and then deliberate with the other jurors, all the while keeping in mind how terrible it would be to convict an innocent person and, conversely, how terrible it would be to acquit, or free, a guilty person, who might well go on to hurt someone else.

CHAPTER FIVE

CIVIL JURY TRIALS

A civil case is usually brought in the name of a person or business. It involves the asking of *damages* (usually money) of another person or business because of wrongdoing, negligence, or breach of duty. For example, Paul Noggin is suing Judy Sebold for damages sustained in a car accident, and Jenny Higgins is suing Dr. Ted Gust for incorrectly diagnosing her heart condition. The party that starts the case is called the plaintiff. The party being sued is the defendant.

A jury that will hear a civil case may contain fewer than the usual twelve members required in criminal cases. Many civil juries, by agreement between attorneys, have only six members. Another big difference is that a civil jury does not have to reach a unanimous decision, as is required in a criminal case. That means the court can accept a verdict agreed upon by five of the six jurors, or ten of the twelve jurors who are deciding the case—and an even smaller number if the parties consent.

Another difference between criminal and civil trials is the way

lawyers conferring outside a courthouse

an attorney can agree to be paid a percentage of any jury award. This is called a contingency fee, and the lawyer does not get paid if the plaintiff does not get an award. It is believed that this practice allows people with little money but excellent grounds for a lawsuit to hire a lawyer. Some people, however, believe this practice encourages lawyers to start questionable suits in the hopes of settling the case before trial or using their trial techniques to persuade a naive jury.

Because a person's freedom is at stake in a criminal case, jurors who decide that type of case must make their decision according to the highest burden of proof, which means the person must be found guilty beyond a reasonable doubt. In civil cases, because the consequences are less severe, the burden of proof need not be as high as in a criminal trial.

Civil cases may require one of two other burdens. The lower burden requires that the jury be satisfied "by the greater weight of the credible evidence." This means that when the jury weighs all the evidence for one side against all the evidence for the other side, one side comes out on top.

In some civil jury trials jurors must use a "middle" burden of proof. The plaintiff in such a case would be required to show proof that is "clear, satisfactory, and convincing." This type of proof is required in cases of fraud, undue influence (usually associated with heirs contesting a will), punitive damages, and any cases arising out of acts that could also be the basis of a criminal suit.

The concept of burden of proof is a difficult one for jurors (as well as some lawyers and judges) to understand. Here's an example to help make it clearer. Larry Reddin, a teacher in a middle school, discovers that his valuable antique watch is missing from his desk. He suspects one of his students, Greg Herman, of stealing it. If the district attorney (representing the state) brings charges against Greg, the evidence must meet the highest burden of proof. The jurors must believe beyond a reasonable doubt that Greg took the watch.

If Larry Reddin starts his own civil suit against Greg to recover the cost of the watch, the jurors in that civil case need only be persuaded by the greater weight of the credible evidence that Greg took the watch and he should be made to pay for it.

Changing our facts slightly, let's assume Reddin sends a letter to a local newspaper, which gets printed and which accuses Greg of being a thief and a criminal and suggests that he has committed other thievery. If Greg sues him for libel (harming his reputation), he must show the jury evidence that reaches the middle burden of proof—evidence that is clear, satisfactory, and convincing. As you can see by comparing the three burdens of proof, the more serious the consequences of the alleged wrongdoing, the stronger the case must be.

Like criminal juries, civil juries decide questions of fact first, but then, unlike criminal juries, they may inquire into other areas. For example, in the case discussed earlier, Paul Noggin versus Judy Sebold, Paul claims that Judy did not yield the right of way at an intersection where there were no stop signs or stoplights. Paul and Judy were both badly hurt as a result of the accident. In Judy Sebold's answer to Paul's "complaint," Judy maintains that Paul told the police he was looking in his glove compartment when they collided. Paul claims that Judy was drinking wine at a friend's house shortly before the accident and that she was drunk and negligent.

After the jury hears all the evidence it must decide who is telling the truth. In some states, it may decide both drivers are to blame for the accident. In that case, the next task will be to "apportion" (divide) the guilt between them. This is called the *comparative negligence rule*. A percentage amount (of blame) is usually assigned to each driver, with the total equaling 100 percent.

In our example, the jury may find that both Paul and Judy were negligent. It then could find Paul 25 percent negligent and Judy 75 percent negligent. In cases with multiple plaintiffs or multiple defendants, this is a very time-consuming job.

Next, jurors in our hypothetical case would probably have to decide how much Paul suffered in damages, that is, how much money Paul has lost as a result of this accident. These questions usually deal with medical and doctor bills, lost wages, and pain and suffering.

In relation to the medical bills, the jury would have to decide whether all or part of Paul's doctor and medical bills were a result of this accident. Judy's lawyer might argue that Paul made his injuries worse by bowling every week. She might also show that, despite doctor's orders, Paul didn't always follow through on the therapy.

Paul is also suing for lost wages. Judy's lawyer might argue that he went to Florida for two weeks on vacation and that this time should be deducted from any award.

Probably the toughest task for any jury is to assign an amount of money to compensate Paul for pain and suffering. The jury is instructed to consider the type of injury, the length of the disability, and the humiliation and embarrassment it has caused. The jury must also take into account how the injury impaired the person's ability to enjoy or carry out his or her normal activities, hobbies, etc.

Sometimes jurors are required to assess future damages. This would occur in our theoretical case if Paul made a claim for "permanency." The jurors must predict how long the person is going to live; how much pain the injured party is going to have in the future; how much he or she will have to spend for medical bills; and how much he or she might have earned were it not for the accident.

Once the jury has decided all of these questions, it is up to the judge to determine the effect of their verdict. That is, the judge will determine if the award given by the jury will be paid to the plaintiff or if the law requires no award to be paid. In rare instances, the judge may actually change the jury's decisions. Generally, jurors have not been allowed to know the effect of their verdict. For example, even if Paul is found 60 percent negligent and Judy only 40 percent, Paul may not recover anything.

Civil trials can be very long and complicated. Some may last a year or more. The jurors may also have to hear highly technical testimony. In the case of *Jenny Higgens* v. *Dr. Ted Gust,* the jurors had to listen to doctors testifying for both the plaintiff and the defendant. In legal jargon, these are called *expert witnesses.* The plaintiff's doctors testified that Dr. Gust made a mistake in treating Jenny which the average cardiologist (heart doctor) would not have made. Dr. Gust's doctors stated that Dr. Gust did what any reasonable, skilled physician would have done when faced with the same facts. As you can see, jurors must take a crash course in medicine before they can intelligently come up with a verdict.

In some recent civil cases, there have been so many parties to the action (plaintiffs and defendants) that the judges have had to rent larger quarters. In one such case in Milwaukee, Wisconsin, in which the plaintiffs were suing numerous drug companies, the judge had to make arrangements to rent an arena!

Besides being complex, civil cases have become expensive for both those bringing the suit and those defending themselves against one. It is not unusual for trials to cost $8,000 to $10,000 dollars or more in expenses. Most of this money is spent on preparation, investigation, depositions of experts, and exhibits. Imagine spending $8,000 on the preparation of your case and not winning! Adding to your woes would be the fact that you would have to pay a portion of the defendant's costs, too. This fact alone has led to an

A lawyer and his clients discuss their trial. The books behind the lawyer contain descriptions and decisions of past cases. This information is used in preparing new cases.

increase in cases submitted to *arbitration,* which means that a professional arbitrator not connected to either side listens to the case and decides it.

The following are some examples of the types of cases tried in civil court:

Product liability cases, in which someone is suing a manufacturer for allowing a product to leave the factory in a defective condition. Examples of these cases are the suits started against several pharmaceutical houses by women who took medication during pregnancy and gave birth to babies with birth defects.

Medical or *legal malpractice* cases, in which the patient or client claims the professional was negligent (did not offer standard care) in handling their treatment or case.

Intentional torts, which are suits started in the civil courts for actions that might be prosecuted criminally, too. It is not unusual to have a person charged with a crime by the state have a corresponding civil case brought by the victim seeking monetary damages. *Battery* (physical violence inflicted against a person) and *false imprisonment* are two of the most common intentional torts.

Occasionally someone may sue a newspaper or radio or TV station because of an article or broadcast they think was known to be false and was used for malicious purposes. This is a *libel* or *slander* suit. A libel suit accuses someone of wrongfully injuring a person's reputation in a written, published work; a slander suit accuses someone of wrongfully injuring someone's reputation by the spoken word.

Many disputes between businesses are also tried in the civil courts.

In the future, the nature of civil trials could change drastically. If the technology becomes affordable, future jurors will probably watch the live testimony of witnesses who are miles from the courtroom. This will greatly aid in the scheduling of cases as well as in making it easier for people to testify.

CHAPTER SIX

WE THE JURY

Officials in each county or state are responsible for finding a "pool" of prospective jurors each week. They must try to find a large enough, randomly selected group of people to meet the needs of the courts. Attorneys for both sides of a case must be able to question enough prospective jurors to feel sure they will be able to pick a jury that can fairly judge the case.

The challenge, then, for the court system is how to locate large numbers of people who would be eligible to serve on juries. Many places use lists of registered voters and randomly pick names. Some also use lists of people who have driver's licenses.

Who is eligible to be a prospective juror? In the early years of this country, a prospective juror had to (1) be a man; (2) own property; (3) pay taxes; and (4) be a voter. These restrictions on jury service effectively banned women and many minorities. Amazingly, women were automatically excluded from juries in some states as recently as 1975; at that time, the U.S. Supreme Court ruled that people could not be excluded on the basis of sex alone.

An exclusively male jury. At one time women and many minorities were not allowed to serve as jurors.

Generally, today, a person must be (1) a citizen of the United States; (2) at least eighteen years old; and (3) able to read and understand the English language. As we shall see, the modern trend is to enable as many people as possible to serve on juries, and to recruit jurors from all age groups, occupations, and racial heritages. In addition, there is a growing body of law that prohibits some past practices that were designed to reduce the number of minorities available for jury service.

Who is not eligible today to be a prospective juror? A person who has been convicted of a serious crime and who has not been officially pardoned is not eligible. In some places, a person who is a party to a lawsuit currently pending in the local courts cannot serve on a jury while the case is open. These are called *automatic exclusions*.

Some people who are eligible to serve on a jury may not be able to. When people are notified that they must report for *jury duty*, they may ask to be excused, explaining why they think they should be. But they must answer the summons to report and be officially excused or they could be found in contempt of court or fined.

People who would certainly be excused from jury duty are those who are very sick or who are physically unable to travel to the courthouse. Blind and deaf people would be excused, as would parents with small children who have no one else to care for them. People who had already served on jury duty during the previous year or two would also probably be excused. Most states have laws concerning how often a person must serve on jury duty.

Many people ask to be excused from jury duty because it would be inconvenient for them or for their employers. It used to be easy to get excused from jury duty merely by saying that your work was "too important" or by having your employer complain that your absence would be a hardship for the company. That is changing. It is becoming more and more difficult to get excused because it would interfere with your work. However, courts are usually willing to postpone a person's jury service to a more convenient time.

Court officials recognize the fact that jury service can be very difficult or disruptive for people. It can also be a financial hardship. Although jurors are paid a small fee for each day that they serve, if they are not paid their regular wage while they are on jury duty, they will probably lose money. But the importance of having an adequate number of eligible and impartial jurors available to the courts each day cannot be ignored. Many changes in the requirements for jury service have been made in recent years to try to balance these competing concerns. One of the major changes has been to shorten the time that prospective jurors must be available to serve.

Over the years, the length of time people have been required to serve on jury duty has steadily gone down from several months at a time to only one or two weeks. Some counties or states now require only "one day or one trial." That means that if a prospective juror appears on a certain day and is not picked for a jury, he or she is finished serving. If the person is picked for a jury, he or she will be finished as soon as the trial is over.

Another major challenge for court officials is to make sure that minorities are properly represented. A jury should represent a true cross section of its community whenever possible, in terms of racial heritage, age, and economic level.

Many handicapped people do not want to be excused from jury duty. They value the public service that jurors perform and do not want to be denied the opportunity to serve their community. However, special accommodations must be made to allow these people to serve as jurors. For example, a deaf person who wants to be considered a potential juror would need an interpreter.

When a prospective juror is not disqualified or excused, he or she must appear at the specified time and date in a jury assembly room with other prospective jurors. A judge or other court official explains the duties and responsibilities that jurors have and the general court procedures they will have to know. Then they wait to be called to a courtroom for actual jury selection.

Many prospective jurors find that the time they spend waiting is terribly boring, especially if they did not bring anything to read. Some people bring needlework or crossword puzzles to help them pass the time. The waiting time can be especially frustrating if they do not know what is causing the delays.

When a judge is ready to start a jury trial, he or she notifies the court officers in the jury assembly room. One of the officers calls the names of prospective jurors who will be sent to the courtroom. Normally, twenty-five or more prospective jurors are sent out for a criminal case in which twelve jurors will be needed. Approximately fifteen people are sent to a courtroom for a civil case that will be heard by six jurors. As many as a hundred people might be needed for a case of first-degree murder because it is hard to find twelve people who are able to be sequestered, or kept apart from everyone else, for many days or weeks. A list of the jurors' names is given to the judge and to each of the attorneys on either side of the case.

Once the prospective jurors are seated in the courtroom, the jury selection process—called *voir dire,* which is French for "to speak the truth"—begins. The process varies a little from place to place, but in all instances the judge and the attorneys ask each prospective juror questions which he or she must answer truthfully. (In federal court cases, only the judge asks questions of prospective jurors. This practice has been criticized by those who believe it is very important for the lawyers on each side to get involved in the voir dire process.) The questions are at first very

A prospective juror passes the time by reading a newspaper.

Attorneys confer with the judge during jury selection for a trial in a state district court. One man is being questioned, while the other prospective jurors await their turn.

general: Where in the city or county do you live? What do you do for a living? Do you know the judge or the attorneys or any of the witnesses involved in this case? Have you ever been a victim of a crime? Is there any reason why you would not be able to fairly judge this case?

The lawyers listen to each prospective juror's answers and take notes. During the voir dire process, some prospective jurors are *struck,* or eliminated, "for cause." This means that the judge and the lawyers for both sides agree that this prospective juror might not be totally fair or objective. For example, someone who is related to one of the attorneys or who is a close friend of one of the parties or one of the witnesses might have strong feelings about the case before hearing any of the evidence. Asking them to be impartial would be asking the impossible. Some people, because of their religion, feel that they can't sit in judgment of another person; they believe that only God can judge people's actions. And, some people feel that they could not be fair serving on a jury in a particular kind of case:

"My son was an armed robbery victim three years ago; he still has nightmares about it. I can't put that out of my mind when I hear about someone who has been held up with a gun."

"I was hurt in a car accident and the insurance company ripped me off. I think that all insurance companies care about is the almighty dollar."

"I'm a secretary in the police department. I don't think they ever arrest innocent people."

After asking general questions, the lawyers look for more specific and personal information. What are the juror's values? Which way would he lean in deciding the facts of the case? Is she liberal and softhearted? Or is she conservative and "law-and-order"?

"Mr. Jensen, you said you were hospitalized within the past five years. Why were you in the hospital? Were you satisfied with your treatment?'' (The lawyer is trying to find out if any prospective jurors have had bad experiences with doctors or a hospital.)

"Ms. Ellis, have you ever filed a claim with your automobile insurance company? Were you at fault in the accident? Do you think your insurance company was fair to you?" (The lawyer is trying a case that involves a young man injured in an automobile accident and wants to find out if prospective jurors have any strong feelings about insurance claims.)

"Mr. Rothstein, have you ever been intoxicated to the point where you couldn't remember anything that occurred?" (The lawyer is trying to find out how prospective jurors feel about a case involving a drunk driver.)

Some voir dire questions involve very sensitive issues that many people would be reluctant to discuss in public, such as a previous arrest. A prospective juror may not want to answer questions about sexual behavior in front of everyone else, for example, "Do you have any feelings about homosexuals?" Because talking about these things can be embarrassing for some people, the judge may allow the lawyers to question the prospective jurors in private.

Even though the other prospective jurors are strangers and will probably never see each other again, the voir dire process can be difficult. For example, it can be very uncomfortable to admit in public that you have been convicted of drunken driving or that you are really prejudiced against some classes of people. It can also be hard not to feel rejected or inadequate if you don't get picked for a jury. You might feel you weren't "good" enough or smart enough or that the lawyers didn't like you.

When the voir dire questions are finished, the lawyers for each side get a chance to strike—for no specified reason—prospective jurors they don't want on the jury. These are called *peremptory strikes*. Each side may take turns eliminating prospective jurors until they have the number they need for the jury. This process was designed to let the lawyers "weed out" people they think will not be sympathetic to their side.

Many lawyers have theories about the kinds of people that would make "good" jurors or "bad" jurors, depending on the kind of case they are trying. For example, a lawyer defending someone who has been accused of committing a crime might try to strike police officers and crime victims. The prosecutor might try to strike social workers and people who have friends that have been in jail. A lawyer suing an insurance company might feel that women would be more sympathetic than men; the lawyer for the insurance company might want businesspeople and others whom they think will be "tough." However, lawyers are strictly forbidden from eliminating people just because of race.

How to select a "good" jury has become the subject of a growing body of psychological research. More and more lawyers hire psychologists or consultants to sit with them in court during the voir dire process and advise them as to which prospective jurors they should strike and which ones they should try to keep on the jury. The use of psychologists or consultants to help a lawyer pick a jury adds considerably to the cost of trying a case and is used only in the most serious of cases. However, it might be another trend for the future.

When a judge begins a jury trial in a serious or complex case that will last more than a few days, he or she may ask that "alternate" jurors be selected. Instead of picking twelve jurors to hear the case, for example, the lawyers choose fourteen or more. All fourteen people hear all of the evidence and all of the arguments. When both sides "rest," or finish their case presentations, two names may be randomly picked by the judge, who then dismisses these people from jury service. The remaining twelve people form the jury that will deliberate and decide the case. Sometimes alternates are chosen at the start.

Alternate jurors are used to make sure that there will be a full jury when the case presentations are finished. Having alternates is a safeguard against someone getting sick or being called home for a family emergency during the trial. Recently, some judges have experimented with the idea of allowing the alternates to join the deliberations but not vote.

If you get picked for a case, listening to the case demands your complete concentration. In a long and complicated case, you may have to struggle to pay attention and stay interested and concerned. Particularly difficult may be the long periods of time outside the courtroom waiting for the trial to start again after a recess or a lunch break, or after the jury is asked to leave so the lawyers can argue some legal question that the jury is not allowed to hear. You may wonder what is going on in the courtroom. If the wait is especially long, you may wonder if the judge and the lawyers are really working or just wasting your time.

When the case presentation is finished, the jury begins deliberations. Being part of a group decision-making process can be very frustrating or very intimidating. You may feel strongly, for example, that one of the witnesses was lying, but several of the other jurors are relying heavily on that witness's testimony. It can be very frustrating to try to convince someone that you are right and he or she is wrong. If you are shy or not very self-confident, it can be very hard to assert yourself and try to convince the rest of the jurors to seriously consider and weigh a piece of evidence that you consider important. The discussions and decisions you must participate in as part of a jury are especially hard because of how important the outcome will be. When the jury finally reaches a verdict, or decides it cannot reach a verdict, each of you individually (and as a group) has to take responsibility for the decisions you make by affirming your verdict to the defendant in court.

Perhaps the most difficult decision is to declare yourself a

During a trial, the jury listens to a prosecutor arguing the case.

"hung" jury, or one that has not been able to reach a decision. How do you think you would feel if you had to walk back into that courtroom to tell the judge that the jury could not reach a unanimous verdict after many, many hours of deliberation? A hung jury means that the victim's family will have to go through trial preparation again; another jury will have to go through the same experience you had.

After the verdict is delivered, the judge dismisses the jury. Depending on how long the trial lasted and the rules governing the length of your jury service, you will either be free to leave or will have to report back to the jury assembly room. If your time of jury service isn't over, you may be picked to hear another case.

Sometimes lawyers want to talk to jurors after a case is finished in order to find out why they reached the decision they did. These lawyers believe the feedback may help them learn what the strong points were in their presentation and what they could have done better. People who have served on a jury can decide whether they want to talk to the lawyer or not.

Serving on a jury can be many different things to different people. It can be inconvenient, frustrating, intimidating, or boring. It can be exciting, interesting, challenging, and even fun. But it is undoubtedly one of the most important things you will ever do as a citizen.

CHAPTER SEVEN

SPECIAL USES OF THE JURY

As you have read, jury trials have been in existence a long time. The most common uses of the jury are in criminal and civil cases—the so-called "petit" jury. But there are and have been some other uses of the jury system.

GRAND JURY

Probably the next most common use of the jury is in the *grand jury* system. Grand juries date back to the twelfth century, when they were used by the king. The king may have introduced the grand jury to counter the growing power of the barons. The king felt then, as do many people today, that requiring criminal complaints to first be heard and accepted as valid by a group of citizens—other than those who would sit in judgment—would act as a safeguard against overzealous prosecutors or those who want to jail their political enemies. Today the grand jury system is still used in about twenty-five states and in our federal courts.

The most distinguishing feature of the grand jury is its function. Grand jurors accuse people of crimes, while trial jurors decide whether accused people are innocent or guilty of these crimes. But there are other differences.

A grand jury is used only in criminal matters and is especially effective in organized crime and corruption investigations. Unlike trial jurors, grand jurors can—in theory—control the investigation and determine the witnesses they see and use a *subpoena* (an order signed by a judge requiring the presence of someone or something in court) to get witnesses to testify. Grand juries usually have more members than trial juries (somewhere between twelve and twenty-three), and the procedure for a grand jury is unlike that of a regular jury trial. Grand jurors are not required to follow the rules of evidence, nor are any lawyers (except for the prosecutor) allowed to participate. Grand juries also operate in secret. And there is no requirement that the grand jury be unanimous in its findings; only a majority need agree. The main question the grand jurors must ask themselves is: "Is there enough evidence to indict, or charge, someone?" Grand jurors don't decide on guilt or innocence; they are required only to find "probable cause" that a crime was committed and who might have committed it. If the grand jury decides there is enough evidence to justify criminal charges, it produces a formal written accusation called an *indictment*.

A juror in a trial jury will usually serve only as long as the trial continues, while a grand juror is empowered to investigate many criminal actions for up to eighteen months. This can be extended in special circumstances for an even longer time. Some of the famous gangsters of the 1930s and many so-called Mafia (organized crime) leaders of recent times were originally investigated and indicted by grand juries.

Today, the grand jury system is coming under increased scrutiny. Some groups believe that grand jurors are too dependent on the prosecutor and that their investigations are, in actuality, controlled by the prosecutor. Also, there have recently been some isolated cases of abuse by the Federal Bureau of Investigation (FBI) and the Internal Revenue Service (IRS) in acquiring otherwise unobtainable documents through the use of a grand jury. This has resulted in a review of grand jury procedures.

INQUESTS

Another jury that investigates, rather than finds guilt or innocence, is the *coroner's jury*—sometimes called an *inquest*. Inquest juries were also part of the early English system. An inquest is held when someone dies under unusual or unknown circumstances and wrongdoing may be suspected. If a body is discovered in the basement of an empty house with the arms and legs tied together and the hands cut off, an inquest would probably be ordered. The inquest, or coroner's jury, listens to all the witnesses who know anything about the death. The procedures for inquests differ from state to state, but normally the district attorney will decide what witnesses to call.

Inquest jurors function in a manner similar to grand jurors. They don't decide the ultimate outcome but rather they make recommendations as to what or who might have caused the death. If they are given sufficient information, they may even recommend to the district attorney that a particular person be charged with a crime. Inquest juries, like criminal juries but unlike grand juries, must be unanimous in their findings. In order to recommend a criminal charge, they must find probable cause—evidence that points to a strong probability that a crime occurred.

SHERIFF'S JURY

In some states the law (usually called a *statute*) allows for sheriffs to call a jury. This jury's function is to decide who is the rightful owner of property seized by the sheriff under court order (sometimes called a *writ of execution*). Many people may claim to be the owner. Another kind of sheriff's jury is a jury started on a *writ of inquiry*. In this jury—again, a jury that came into existence by statute—the jurors would be required to decide how much to give someone for damages. Although this is normally done in a civil trial, with both sides arguing the case, in this situation the jury is required to play the role of a defendant who has failed to answer the suit.

CONDEMNATION JURY

Another jury created by law and not in existence everywhere is the *condemnation jury*. This jury decides how much money a landowner is entitled to get when his or her land is condemned for public use and taken away. If Allister Ferguson owns a farm, and the highway department decides to build an expressway through his cornfield, he could ask a jury to decide how much the state should pay him for the land the state takes for the road.

STRUCK JURY

The *struck jury,* or specifically selected jury, came into existence in ancient times. It was custom then to collect the names of all the knights and important people in the vicinage (area) who would later be called on for jury trials dealing with important issues or where notorious people were involved. Although this type of jury was imported, it is out of fashion in our country, where we consider everyone equal and where we have no nobility. It may remain "on the books" in some places, but it is never used.

ADVISORY JURY

In some states the law allows a judge to impanel a jury in certain cases in which the parties would ordinarily not be entitled to a jury. This may happen in some civil cases in which there are multiple causes of action, some of which entitle the person to a jury. In this instance, a judge may use an *advisory jury* to decide all the issues.

Another use of an advisory jury is for very controversial cases or issues in which the judge may want the benefit of the wisdom and experience of others. The judge will impanel a jury and get its input, but then he or she will be responsible for rendering the final decision.

GLOSSARY OF LEGAL TERMS

Action. The legal, formal name given to the issues embodied in a complaint against another.

Alibi. A reason why a defendant could not have done what he or she is accused of doing; usually a statement by a witness that the defendant was somewhere else.

Appeals Court (also called **Appellate Court**). A court that reviews decisions made by trial courts because one side in a case is unhappy with the decision and asks for a "second opinion" on review; an appeals court can agree with the trial court and uphold the lower court decision or disagree with the lower court and overturn the decision.

Arbitration. The process in which the parties on both sides of a dispute agree to allow an impartial person (an arbitrator) to settle the dispute as an alternative to a trial.

Award. An official decision by a judge or jury that one party must pay another party a specific amount of money.

Bailiff. The law enforcement officer responsible for order and security in a courtroom; also responsible to watch over and assist the jury.

Bench. The place in the courtroom where the judge sits; also, the court itself.

Burden of Proof. The amount of evidence required in a case in order for the jury to find in favor of the person bringing the suit; the more serious the consequences of the case, the greater amount of proof required.

Change of Venue. A request of a judge by a party to a lawsuit for a different place of trial or a jury from outside the local area; usually, this request is made because it would be difficult or impossible to pick a fair and impartial jury from the place where the case was filed because there has been so much pre-trial publicity.

Circumstantial Evidence. Any statement or object presented in a court case as proof of a fact that could lead a reasonable person to infer that something happened or someone did something; indirect evidence.

Civil Case. A legal action started against another asking recovery for a private wrong; not a criminal case.

Closing Arguments. The opportunity given to the lawyers at the close of testimony to sum up what they believe the jury's verdict should be.

Complaint. In civil cases, the legal document that states the reasons why someone is being sued and the relief sought, for example, monetary damages or return of property. In criminal cases, the legal document that states the law (or laws) broken and the reasons why the person (or persons) named in the complaint is accused of committing a crime.

Criminal Case. A legal action started by a state or federal prosecutor in the name of the state or the United States against a person accused of committing a public wrong (a crime) and asking for a prescribed punishment.

Cross-Examination. Questioning of a witness by the lawyer who did not call the witness.

Damages. Monetary compensation for injuries, harm, or loss that can be recovered in a court action.

Defendant. A person in a trial who is accused of a crime or some wrongdoing.

Defense Attorney. A lawyer who acts on behalf of a defendant on trial.

Deliberations. A jury's discussion and evaluation of the evidence presented in a trial.

Deposition. A written or videotaped record of a statement made, under oath, by a witness outside of a courtroom to be used during a trial so the witness will not have to be present.

Direct Evidence. Any statement or object presented in a court case as proof of a fact, without the need for any additional information to prove the fact, for example, eyewitness testimony.

District Attorney. The prosecutor in a trial. See **Prosecutor**.

Evidence. Any statement or object presented in a court case as proof of a fact. See also **Circumstantial Evidence** and **Direct Evidence**.

Exhibit. A document, photograph, or other relevant object presented to the court during a trial.

Expert Witness. A person who has specialized knowledge or experience in some area who can testify as a recognized authority about certain facts or opinions. An expert witness need not have firsthand knowledge of the facts and can answer hypothetical questions.

Finding. A decision made by a judge or jury.

Foreperson. Chairperson on a jury; a person who leads or organizes the discussion of a jury and is responsible for trying to keep order.

Grand Jury. A jury that investigates criminal complaints and decides whether someone should be formally charged with committing a crime.

Hung Jury. A jury that cannot agree on a verdict; this can result in a new trial before different jurors.

Impanel a Jury. The act of officially selecting a pool of people to serve as jurors in a case.

Indictment. A formal written accusation prepared for a court by a grand jury; it outlines what crime or crimes are believed to have been committed, and names the person or persons who probably committed those crimes.

Intentional Tort. A violent act committed by someone who intended harm to be done. The opposite of an accident.

Judiciary. The judicial branch of government; a system of courts of justice; judges as a group.

Jury. A group of people who have sworn to decide the facts in a court case and to reach a fair verdict, or decision.

Mistrial. A trial that ends without a final decision because some error has been made. For example, the jury has heard or seen something they should not have. Also, a trial that ends without a final decision because the jury cannot agree on a verdict. See also **Hung Jury.**

Motion. A request for a judge to make a decision on some legal issue raised in a case.

Oath. A formal promise to perform a specific duty or act.

Objection. A request by a lawyer during a trial that the judge order a witness not to answer a question asked by the other lawyer. The judge must either "sustain" the objection (agree with it and forbid the witness to answer it) or "overrule" it (allow the question to be asked).

Opening Statements. The presentation made by the lawyers on each side of a case at the start of a trial. During opening statements the issues and facts that will be presented are outlined;

the purpose of opening statements is to give the jury an overview of the case so the jurors will be better able to understand the evidence they will hear.

Party. A person who is named in a legal action as either one of the people starting the action or one of the people responding to a legal suit; usually the plaintiff or the defendant.

Peremptory Strikes. Prospective jurors who are eliminated by the lawyers on each side after voir dire because the lawyer prefers another juror; no reason has to be given for these strikes.

Plaintiff. A person who starts an action, files a complaint, or sues another person.

Plea Bargain. A criminal court practice that allows someone charged with a crime to plead guilty to a lesser offense (so there will be no trial) or allows them to plead guilty to the original charge with the prosecutor promising to recommend a particular sentence.

Pleadings. Formal written statements of the positions taken by the parties in a lawsuit.

Probable Cause. Evidence that points to a strong likelihood that a crime occurred or that a specific person committed a crime.

Prosecutor. The government official who is authorized to accuse and prosecute (bring to trial) someone who is believed to have committed a crime. Prosecutors are known by various names in different places—i.e., district attorney, state's attorney, and people's attorney.

Public Defender. In criminal cases, a lawyer who is appointed and paid by the state or federal government to defend a person who has been accused of committing a crime and who is not able to afford a private attorney.

Restitution. Money that is paid, or ordered by a judge to be paid, to a crime victim to compensate for losses suffered as a result of a crime. Used mainly as a condition of probation.

Rest One's Case. An announcement by a lawyer that he or she has finished presenting the evidence for that side.

Sentence. In criminal cases, the decision by a judge or jury as to what punishment is appropriate for a convicted defendant.

Sequestering. Keeping a jury apart from other people and prohibiting members from reading or hearing news accounts of the case they are hearing.

Subpoena. An order signed by a judge or prosecutor requiring the presence of someone or something (i.e., records) in a court on a specific date and time.

Suit. A lawsuit; an action started by one party against another to recover losses believed to have been caused by the second party.

Summons. An official order issued by a judge or law enforcement official which notifies the person named in the summons that legal action has been started against the person and which tells him or her a date, time, and place he or she must appear to answer the complaint.

Testimony. Evidence given after taking an oath in court to tell the truth; questions answered under oath concerning what one knows about a case being heard in court.

Tort. A private or civil wrong or injury that is not a crime.

Transcript. An official written record of a court proceeding.

Trial. The formal presentation of both sides of a dispute before a jury or a judge.

Verdict. The decision that a jury or judge makes after hearing and considering all of the evidence and testimony in a case.

Voir Dire. A French phrase meaning "to speak the truth." It is the process of questioning prospective jurors before selecting a jury that will hear a case.

Witness. Someone who has seen or heard something; someone who provides evidence about something; someone who is officially ordered to testify in a court.

INDEX

Advisory jury, 85–86
Alternate jurors, 78–79
Ancient times, jury system, 15, 17
Arbitration, 68
Automatic exclusions, 71

Bailiff, 33, 51
Battery cases, 68
Bench, judge's, 33
Burden of proof
    civil cases, 63–64
    criminal cases, 55

Change of venue, 56
Circumstantial evidence, 44, 46

Civil trials, 61–68
    burden of proof, 63–64
    complexity of, 66
    contingency fee of lawyers, 63
    costs of, 66
    damages, 61
    decisions made in, 64–66
    facts presented to jury, 64
    size of jury, 61
    types of cases, 68
Comparative negligence rule, 64
Condemnation jury, 85
Constitution, 10
    on trial by jury, 38
Contingency fee, 63

Coroner's jury, 84
Court clerk, 33
Court reporter, 33
Courtroom
    parts of, 29, 33
    people involved in, 33, 35
    rules of trials, 37
Criminal trials, 52–60
    death penalty decision, 59
    facts presented to, 55–56
    insanity trials, 59–60
    mistrials, 52
    new place for trial, 56–57
    sequestering jurors, 57
    special problems for jurors, 56
Cross examination, 37

Death penalty, 59
Defendant, 33
Defense attorney, 35
Deliberate, 37
Deposition, 44
Direct examination, 37

English system, juries, 17–18, 21–22, 24, 26
Executive branch, 10–11

False imprisonment cases, 68
Foreperson, 51

Gallery, 33

Government
    judiciary, 11, 13, 15
    separation of powers, 9–11
Grand jury, 82–84
    criticisms of, 83–84
    function of, 83
    history of, 82
    indictment, 83
    size of, 83

Handicapped, 72
Hung jury, 52, 81

Indictment, 83
Inquests, 84
Insanity trials, 59–60
Intentional torts, 68

Judiciary, 11, 13, 15
Jurors
    alternate jurors, 78–79
    charging the jury, 48
    decision-making of, 79
    eligibility guidelines, 71
    facts presented to, 44, 46
    finding jurors, 69
    good/bad jurors, 78
    keeping facts of case from, 48, 50
    laws related to, 40
    leader/foreperson, 51
    oath taken by, 40, 43

Jurors (*continued*)
   questions for judge, 50–51
   role of, 43–46
   selection of jury, 73, 76–78
   summons to jury duty, 40
   verdict, delivering, 79, 81
Jury box, 35, 50
Jury duty, 71
   changes in requirements, 72
   people excused from, 71–72
Jury system
   advisory jury, 85–86
   civil trials, 61–68
   criminal trials, 52–60
   grand jury, 82–84
   history of, 15–26
      ancient times, 15, 17
      English system, 17–18, 21–22, 24, 26
   inquests, 84
   sheriff's jury, 84–85
   struck jury, 85
Jury view, 44

Lawyers
   contingency fee, 63
   courtroom, 35
Legislative branch, 11
Libel, 68

Lockup, 37

Malpractice cases, 68
Mistrial, 48, 52

Objection, 37

Petit jury, 82
Plaintiff, 35, 61
Product liability cases, 68
Prosecutor, 33
Public defender, 35
Publicity, and criminal trials, 56

Rules of evidence, 37

Separation of powers, 9–11
Sequestering jurors, 57
Sheriff's jury, 84–85
Statute, 84
Struck jury, 85
Subpoena, 83

Testimony, 33, 37
Transcript, 33

Verdict, 79
Voir dire, 73

Witness stand, 35
Writ of execution, 85
Writ of inquiry, 85